French Fashion Illustrations of the Twenties

634 Cuts from La Vie Parisienne

Edited and Arranged by

Carol Belanger Grafton

Dover Publications, Inc. • New York

Copyright © 1987 by Dover Publications, Inc.
All rights reserved under Pan American and International Copyright Conventions.

Published in Canada by General Publishing Company, Ltd., 30 Lesmill Road, Don Mills, Toronto, Ontario.
Published in the United Kingdom by Constable and Company, Ltd., 10 Orange Street, London WC2H 7EG.

French Fashion Illustrations of the Twenties: 634 Cuts from "La Vie Parisienne" is a new work, first published by Dover Publications, Inc., in 1987.

DOVER *Pictorial Archive* SERIES

Manufactured in the United States of America
Dover Publications, Inc., 31 East 2nd Street, Mineola, N.Y. 11501

Library of Congress Cataloging-in-Publication Data

French fashion illustrations of the twenties.

(Dover pictorial archive series)
1. Fashion—France—History—20th century—Pictorial works.
2. Costume—France—History—20th century—Pictorial works. 3. Vie Parisienne—Illustrations. I. Grafton, Carol Belanger. II. Vie parisienne. III. Title. IV. Series.
GT880.F72   1987   741.67′2′0944   87-13597
ISBN 0-486-25458-5 (pbk.)

Publisher's Note

The Belle Epoque—that flamboyant display of opulence and profligate luxury—was abruptly ended by the First World War. With the Armistice of 1918 came a brief attempt to return fashion to prewar modes, but women had begun to attain a freedom, previously denied them, that was reflected in dress. The figure was no longer restricted by a corset; tubelike dresses allowed a freedom of movement that was suited to the new dance crazes. The waistline dropped and the hemline rose. To compensate for the simplicity of cut, these garments were ornamented with fringes, beading, button and fur trims and other devices. Boldness in the patterning of fabric had begun to be used earlier in the century as a result of the Bakst and Benois designs for Diaghilev's Ballets Russes and the Orientalism of couturier Paul Poiret.

We tend to let the boyish image of the flapper dominate our conception of the twenties. With her bobbed hair, short skirts and flattened chest, she seems the epitome of the age. But in reality the flapper marks only the last few years of the decade. For the main part, fashions were more feminine and sensuous, giving woman the option of revealing or obscuring as much as she wished.

The sheer variety of clothes was itself impressive, ranging from elaborate *robes de style* to pajama suits and a full array of sportswear. Hats tended to be smaller than the enormous creations that had been a feature of the years just before the war, and cloche designs dominated the last years of the twenties. The font of all these styles, was, of course, Paris.

Founded in 1863, the magazine *La Vie Parisienne* assiduously noted the life of the beau monde. Sprinkled among its cartoons, satirical pieces, gossip and fashion news were elegant sketches documenting the latest modes. Although the drawings were unsigned, it is clear that the fashions depicted in them were inspired by such masters as Poiret, Fortuny, Molyneux and Lanvin. They are presented here as a contemporary record of the evolution of the decade's styles.

1918

6   (1918)

1919

1920

14   **(1920)**

16   (1920)

(1920) 23

1921

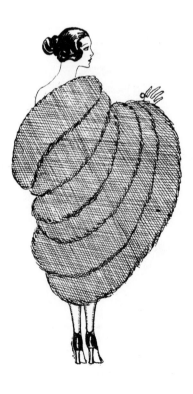

26   **(1921)**

28 **(1921)**

1922

38   (1922)

44   (1922)

1923

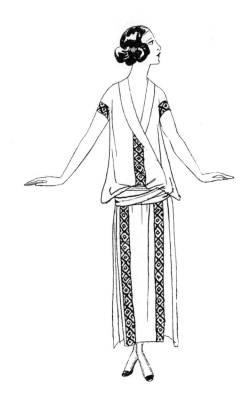

46   **(1923)**

1924

56   **(1924)**

58　**(1924)**

64   (1924)

1925

66   (1925)

68   (1925)

70　**(1925)**

1926

74   (1926)

76   (1926)

1927

82 **(1927)**

84 (1927)

1928

88   (1928)